S0-BQZ-224

DATE DUE

GREAT CARTOONS OF THE WORLD

GREAT
CARTOONS
OF THE WORLD

BY THE WORLD'S FOREMOST CARTOONISTS

EIGHTH SERIES

EDITED BY JOHN BAILEY

CROWN PUBLISHERS, INC., NEW YORK

Acknowledgments and thanks are gratefully
made to the following publishers and cartoonists
for permitting the use of the cartoons appearing in this book:

THE PUBLISHERS:

DAC News, Dikobraz, Editions Denöel, *Look, Medical Economics, Nebelspalter, The New Yorker, Punch*, Roháč, *Saturday Evening Post, Saturday Review.*

THE CARTOONISTS:

Charles Addams, Robert André, Miroslav Barták, George Booth, Adolf Born, Whitney Darrow, Jr., Chon Day, Robert Day, Eldon Dedini, Boris Drucker, Michael ffolkes, John Glashan, Alex Graham, Peter Haas, Stanislav Holý, Stan Hunt, Edward Koren, Lee Lorenz, Charles Martin, Frank Modell, Guillermo Mordillo, Hans Moser, William O'Brian, Bruce Petty, Peter Paul Porges, George Price, Donald Reilly, Vladimir Renčin, Mischa Richter, Al Ross, Charles Saxon, Jean-Jacques Sempé, Vahan Shirvanian, Claude Smith, Leslie Starke, Jules Stauber, William Steig, James Stevenson, Norman Thelwell, Bill Tidy, Barney Tobey, Vlasta Zábranský.

Adolf Born   © 1974 Adolf Born

From time to time various persons are moved to remark that humor cannot be analyzed. But the professional cartoonist has carefully analyzed the several basic gag-structures: *Self-Justification and Rejection* ("If that is right, I am wrong."); *Displacement* ("A martyr is a pile of wood set on fire with a man on top."); the *Opposite* ("Perhaps you have the corset on upside down."); *Play with Words and Love of Non-Reason* (" . . . lead us not into Penn Station."); *Familiarity and Recognition; Resentment of Authority; Incongruity;* and a few others.

These are rapidly absorbed into his subconscious mind and forgotten. Nevertheless, they are there and easily called upon on Tuesday when the cartoonist writes a dozen gags to be shown to the editors on Wednesday. He does this every week, never doubting as he sits down that he will think of twelve gags.

When you ask a cartoonist how he does it, he is unable to tell you, just as the concert pianist is unable to describe to you the hundreds of separate muscle movements he makes in the moment it takes him to run his fingers across the keys and produce an emotion in you—not necessarily laughter, in this case.

The young man who has the knack of being funny, and decides to become a cartoonist, has stumbled on the rules but is quite unaware that he knows them. The chances are that he knows only some of the rules and those imperfectly. He twists what you say into an *opposite*, or carries your idea to an extreme, or hunches up his shoulders and pretends to be George. But he will not be a professional until he learns that the thing he has carried to an extreme will be funnier if it is carried to a greater extreme, and that upon passing the point at which the extreme becomes so great that it can no longer be accepted by his audience as believable it becomes less and less funny; that the *opposite* he has thought of is not an exact opposite, and that if he had thought further he might have been able to combine the *opposite* with one or two other gag-structures into a shining whole that would cause his audience to fall down on the ground with laughter.

Having learned the rules, he would do well to forget them, as you have forgotten the rules for tying your shoelaces. Conscious of the rules, his first imitation of George may lack something, for the same reason that a tennis player learning the rule of not dropping the racket-head knocks the first few balls out of court.

His imitation of George, his cartoon, the caricatured figure in his cartoon, and a word that imitates another word, all share the same basic structure. To learn one is to learn the rest. The laughter they produce involves rejection of them by the audience. They know what George looks like and how he speaks. They see that the imitator looks and sounds like George, and they laugh to announce that they know he is not George, that they see the resemblance, that they get the point.

If one simply looks and sounds like George, the laughter need be merely enough to make them feel *Adequate* again—to let all concerned know, in *Self-Justification*, that they are perfectly familiar with George and that they see the difference between the imitator and George. To construct a better piece of humor something else will have to be added. Thus one exaggerates George's manner of walking or of wearing his hat, or carries to an extreme the sound of his voice or his speech mannerisms. Further, one takes something that everyone knows that George says or thinks and twists it into an *opposite* or carries it to a *logical extreme*.

A word that imitates another word is laughed at for the same reasons. On seeing or hearing the sentence "To purify the city's water it is forced through an aviator," the audience will laugh to announce that the proper word is known to them. If they remained silent those around them might suppose that the proper word was unknown to them. This habit of *Rejection and Self-Justification* is so strong that people will laugh for the same reasons, even when alone.

If the word, or George, or the subject of a cartoon is completely unknown to them they will not laugh. The thing shown must be sufficiently familiar to the reader to enable him to get the point. He must have something to reject. The Scotsman wearing a skirt, or the man with a ponytail, is rejected for a slightly different reason, but *Self-Justification* is involved—"If he is right, then I am wrong"—which is the same reason for which Columbus was rejected and laughed at by people who thought the earth was flat.

The cartoonist begins a cartoon by thinking of a general subject that is familiar to the public and reduces a part of that subject to a statement of fact. This statement of fact is equivalent to a cliché, or to George, or to any common belief or knowledge. *Russia is an unhappy country* may be taken as a statement of fact.

The next step is to reduce the statement of fact to a particular situation. The cartoonist thinks all around the subject, making new and more particular statements of fact about lack of freedom, cheap watches, censorship, the absence of religion, and the fact that Christmas has been done away with—no office parties, no Christmas trees, no Christmas presents, no lights, no turkey.

At this point he realizes that to wish someone a Merry Christmas in Russia is an *opposite*. So far he has a cartoon idea, but no gag. He considers every possible way that a Russian might be wished a Merry Christmas, from a fortune cookie to a sign on the side of a bus. When the capitalistic idea of a vending machine occurs to him he has another *opposite,* and he knows that what he needs in the caption is yet another *opposite* to contrast with the felicitous beginning of the card's message, "Merry Christmas. . . ."

Having got this far, ". . . you poor Communist bastard" flows almost easily from his pen. There is an added undercurrent of amusement in the *incongruity* and indignity of the machine seeming to know that it is handing the guy an appropriate fortune card, and several secondary humor structures are present—*Sarcasm, Superiority, Sympathy*—in the whole idea of anyone living in despair on such a bleak tundra bothering to get weighed at all.

The rest is easy. The cartoonist needs only to: 1. Make a rough sketch of the setting, the character, and the action. 2. Make further sketches of the character, with the idea of improving his position in the space, the attitude of his body, and the gesture. 3. Make a number of sketches of facial expressions, seeking the expression which will reveal to the reader the exact state of the character's mind—which leaves no doubt that his condition is bad enough without being reminded of it.

This is the way a cartoonist spends Tuesday, and I would add a word of caution to the reader. Never speak to a cartoonist on Tuesday.

John Bailey
New York City 1974

George Booth

"Whistle, you dumb bastard!"

© 1973 The New Yorker

Jean-Jacques Sempé

1

4

Charles Martin

2

3

5

6

Charles Addams

"It's going to be tough to top that."

Lee Lorenz

"I need reassurance, Miss Kimball. Send someone in on his hands and knees."

Vlasta Zábranský

" 'Anon' was good enough for your father."

Michael ffolkes

1

2

3

Frank Modell

"And don't think I'm just signing up for defense, Buster."

© 1973 The New Yorker

Eldon Dedini

© 1974 Eldon Dedini

"I heard a bit of good news today.
We shall pass this way but once."

George Price   © 1973 The New Yorker

Norman Thelwell

Stanislav Holý

Dedini

© 1974 Eldon Dedini

KOREN

Edward Koren

"Dickie, I hardly recognized you! You've changed your format."

YOU ARE
HERE

Charles Addams

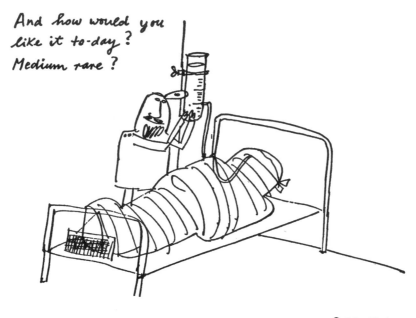

John Glashan

Adolf Born

Robert Day

"Ready for occupancy? Are you sure?"

1

2

Hans Moser

3

© 1974 Hans Moser

Boris Drucker

"I'm taking karate lessons."

© 1974 Boris Drucker

William Steig

1

"He's a lousy golfer, but he always brings a flask."

2

3

4

Guillermo Mordillo   © Guillermo Mordillo

PRIVATE

The
Curiosity
Shop

Norman Thelwell

© Punch

Tobey

"I've often wondered, Agnes—if there was a fire what is the first thing you would save?"

© Barney Tobey

"I hate these one-man shows."

Hans Moser

Donald Reilly

"Well, I think he's great. He's improved building security dramatically, and at Christmas he's delighted with a banana."

Eldon Dedini

"Hello. Are there any hot baths in this neighborhood?"

© 1974 Eldon Dedini

Lee Lorenz

"That crack of yours about his beady little pig eyes was quite uncalled-for."

Jules Stauber

Miroslav Barták

Alex Graham

"Think about it. Your milk, my milk, blended with the milk of God knows how many other cows, making us just objects, destroying our individualism—we become little more than milk machines!"

Eldon Dedini

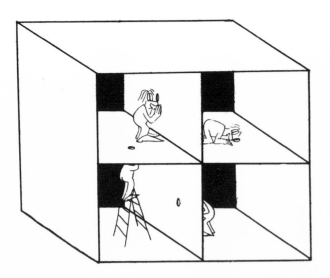

Stanislav Holý

© Dikobraz

Mischa Richter

"Welcome aboard. This is your captain, Margaret Williamson, speaking."

Donald Reilly

"I'll bet it would drive them up the wall if they knew we were out here looking but not buying."

"The typewriter! Lash the typewriter!"

Leslie Starke   © 1974 Punch

Jules Stauber   © Jules Stauber

William Steig

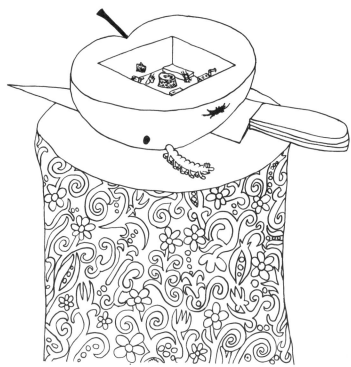

Stanislav Holý

Leslie Starke

James Stevenson

"He's a lousy ballplayer, but he gets along very well with the fans."

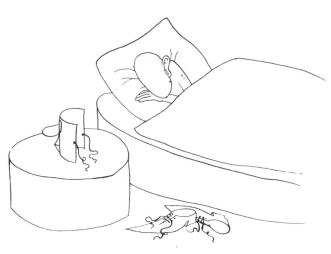

Stanislav Holý

Barney Tobey

"It's impossible to carry on a conversation with that bloody racket Mozart is making."

Stanislav Holý

Chon Day

"My wife takes the Rolls, my daughter takes the Caddie, my son takes the Jag, and I'm left with this damn thing!"

Drucker

Boris Drucker

© Boris Drucker

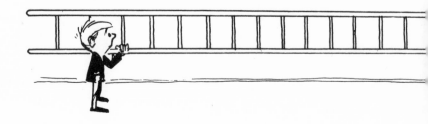

Eldon Dedini

"Please may we have our model aeroplane back?"

Alex Graham

KOREN

Edward Koren

"Paul's got an article in the magazine section, Ann's book is reviewed by Dick, Buddy has a short piece on the Op-Ed page, Roy

has something in the travel section, there's an essay by Norman on Matthew's new movie, and a letter on endangered species by your mother."

Michael ffolkes

"Your father and I are incompatible, that's all."

Eldon Dedini

"Merry Christmas, you poor Communist bastard."

© 1974 Eldon Dedini

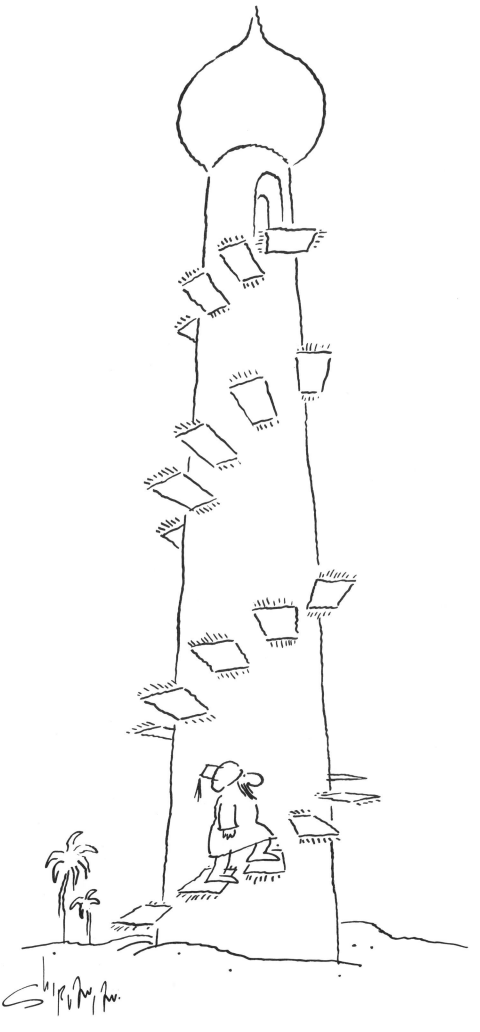

Vahan Shirvanian

Guillermo Mordillo   © Guillermo Mordillo

Charles Martin

"Would you mind, sir, not walking around <u>inside</u> the sculpture?"

© 1974 Charles Martin

Whitney Darrow, Jr.   "Whenever I'm in the dumps, I just sit back and think of my hundred   © 1973 The New Yorker
and fifty million dollars."

Charles Saxon

"When did you start quoting 'Rolling Stone'?"

Norman Thelwell

"That's my favourite—our one hundred thousandth visitor."

1.

2.

3.

4.

5.

thelwell

Petty

Bruce Petty

Peter Paul Porges

"You flunked what?"

Alex Graham   *"I'm through to the semi-final—she dislocated her elbow."*   © 1971 Punch

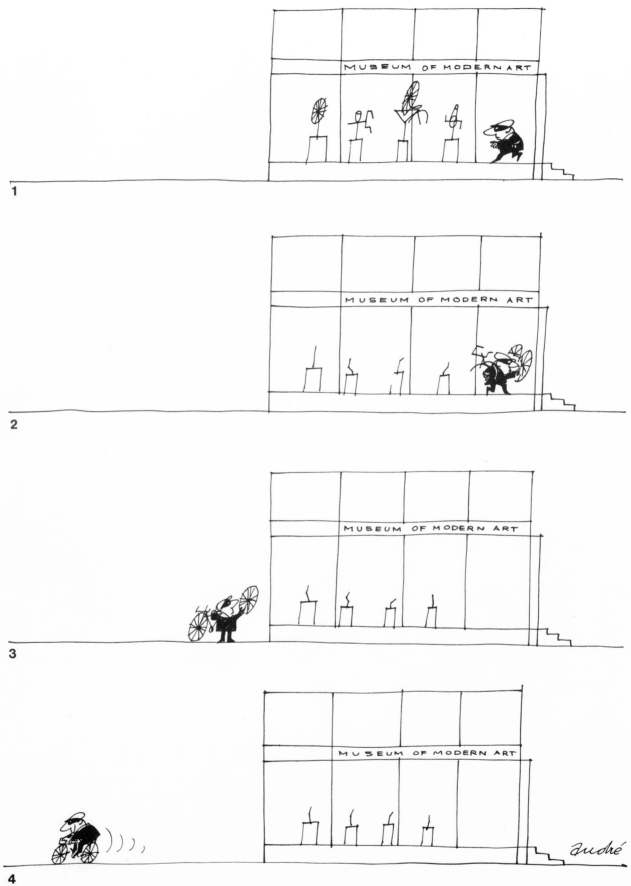

1

2

3

4

Robert André

Stan Hunt   "That's the Beveridge L. Remington the public never sees."

Peter Paul Porges

"The triptych is genuine—it's the cathedral that's fake."

Charles Martin

"You're going to have company, Mr. Erdman."

The Last of the Great Hoarders

by ffolkes

"It's me—Gwendolyn, your wife."

"George has a thing about pâté de foie gras."

"It's the largest private collection of baked beans in the country."

"Oh, no, not another Canaletto!"

ael ffolkes

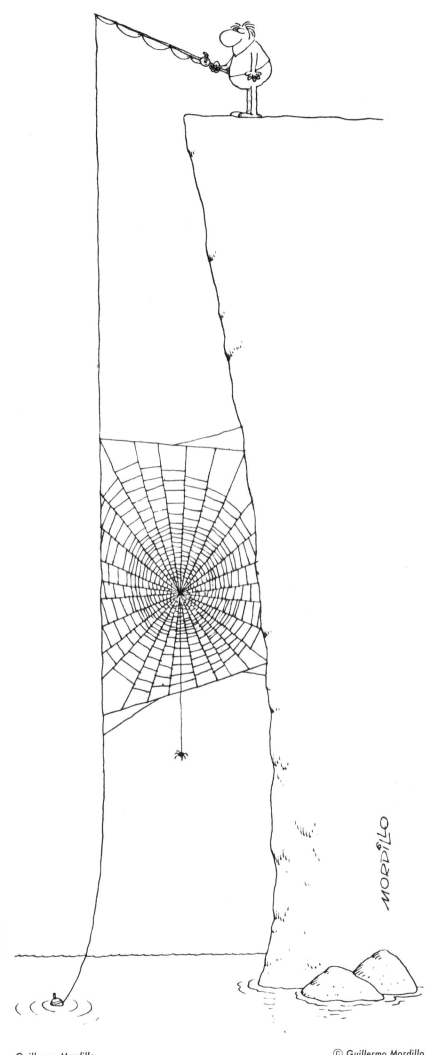

C.E.M.

© 1974 Charles Martin

Guillermo Mordillo

© Guillermo Mordillo

Donald Reilly

"What does it matter if he wears a ponytail, as long as he swiftly completes his appointed rounds?"

© 1973 The New Yorker

Robert Day

"Pinky Russell! Don't tell me <u>you're</u> the last man on earth!"

Stanislav Holý   © Dikobraz

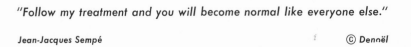

"Follow my treatment and you will become normal like everyone else."

Jean-Jacques Sempé   © Dennël

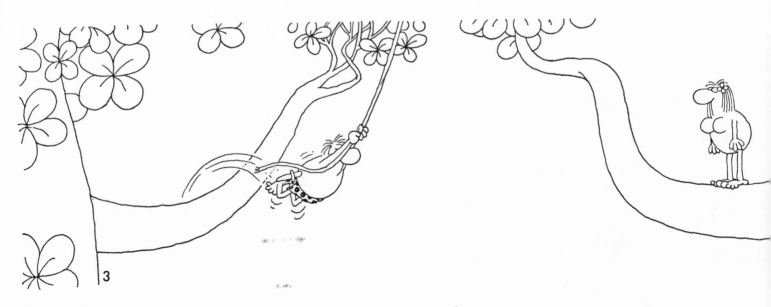

Guillermo Mordillo

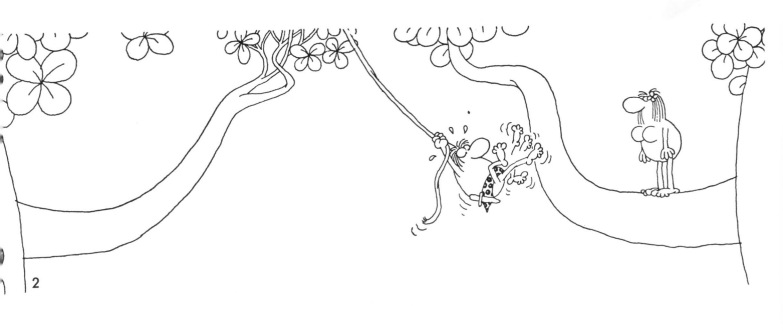

© Guillermo Mordillo

Lee Lorenz   "As an equal-opportunity employer, I have to tell you that you're both fired."

Vlasta Zábranský   © 1972 Roháč

Charles Martin

Boris Drucker   "I _am_ a veteran."   © 1974 Boris Drucker

Boris Drucker

Jean-Jacques Sempé

"What's come over you, George? Are you drunk?"

"What a relief not to have to fiddle around adjusting the flesh tones."

Bill Tidy   *"Thanks, we'll try the north face. It's cheaper."*   © Bill Tidy

William O'Brian

Miroslav Barták   © Dikobraz

OBRIAN

"According to my figures, we could retire right now on an annual income of forty-
eight dollars and fifty cents."

I'm too tired to hit you to-day, instead I'll take you to lunch at an Indian restaurant.

John Glashan   © John Glashan

Frank Modell

Guillermo Mordillo   © Guillermo Mordillo

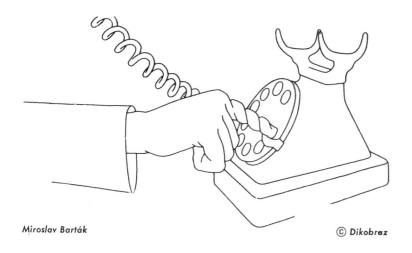

Miroslav Barták

"Bugs! What about bugs?"

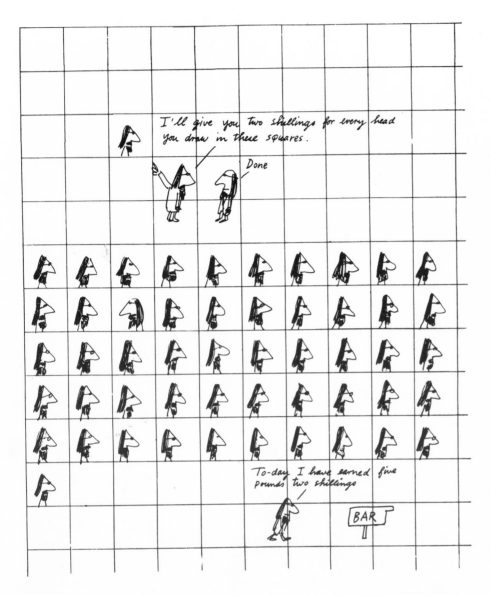

John Glashan

© 1974 John Glashan

Norman Thelwell

"Of course it was never intended for this sort of traffic."

Jean-Jacques Sempé   *"... and to make it worse, you throw me bread, Georgette!"*   © Denoël

man Thelwell

"Attention all shipping!"

Miroslav Barták

© Dikobraz

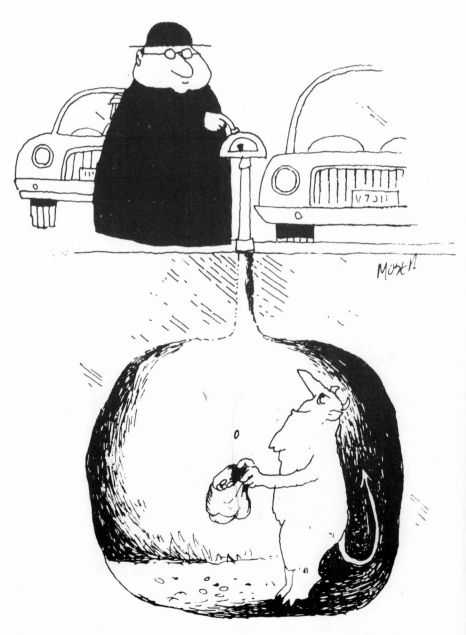

Hans Moser

"Well, I don't call <u>that</u> very intelligent."

Guillermo Mordillo   © Guillermo Mordillo

Eldon Dedini   *"Well, we're on our way, Cheng-Yu. To unlock the secrets of the universe."*   © 1974 Eldon Dedini

Michael ffolkes

"Notre Dame? I'm going that way myself."

Charles Martin

"I'm down here, dear, in Clytemnestra's bedchamber."

C·E·M·

Adolf Born

Miroslav Barták

Jean-Jacques Sempé

"The door!"

© Denoël

"I've found the nicest new doctor. He's fat <u>too.</u>"

Jean-Jacques Sempe
"*Think for a moment, Armand. If there really are beings endowed with a superior intelligence, why would they want to send signals to you?*"

Jules Stauber © Jules Stauber

ffolkes

"We'll probably get prettier girls when they simplify the machines."

Jules Stauber

© Jules Stauber

Leslie Starke

"Your car will be ready in a couple of weeks, sir. Our senior partner
is personally handling the final series of road tests."

© 1974 Punch

George Booth

"Your bill comes to forty-eight dollars more than we estimated, because that little black thing with a lot of wires going into it needed fixing."

Michael ffolkes

"He really <u>must</u> be a pilgrim."

Jean-Jacques Sempé

"Sinking? Do I understand you correctly, Captain? Are you serious?"

© Denoël

Adolf Born

Claude Smith

"Would you care to join us? We're having a family reunion in the dining-room."

1

2

Chon Day   *"I now pronounce you man and wife.
Have a nice day."*

3

4

5

6

DIRECTION

7

8

Robert André

Miroslav Barták

© Dikobraz

Jules Stauber

© Jules Stauber

Barney Tobey

"Sorry, mister, that's not in the sale."

Starving
writer

Powerful Agent

At last
Symington!
I do believe
we've done it
this time..

The
ROLE
of the
AGENT
in the
AWAKENING
TO-MORROW

John Glashan

Naturally, you'll
get nothing
for it —
but think
of the
PRESTIGE

J. Glashan

The Bible didn't earn its advance for nearly
fifteen hundred years

Tell me about your NOVELLA

It's about a millionaire who sails the Caribbean in a converted oil tanker firing Alsation dogs to the Sharks from an adapted depth charge gun ....

He keeps the dogs on their METTLE by feeding them Shark meat ...

. The BLOCK again, dear.?

NO.
Toothache

He's BIG.
As Big as RILKE —
before he Sold Out

John Glashan

The bloody Impertinence ...

TIMES LITERARY SUPPLEMENT

John Glashan

© John Glashan

Eldon Dedini   "We were thinking more along the lines of a bather by Renoir or Degas."   © 1973 The New Yorker

BREAKfast dear!

John Glashan   © John Glashan

Whitney Darrow, Jr.   *"And in the western section I've just put in another six hundred acres of Hamburger*   © 1973 The New Yorker
Helper."

Michael ffolkes

"We can't rule out snake-bite."

© 1974 Michael ff

Jean-Jacques Sempé

"Rodrique is brave, eh? He is virtuous, eh? Would you like me to tell
you how large an allowance he gives me and the children?"

© Denoël

1

2

3

4

5

6

Charles Martin

"So, I am <u>not</u> the first man to scale the Jungspitze."

CEM

© 1974 Charles Martin

Adolf Born

© Dikobraz

Norman Thelwell

"They don't seem to notice the minis."

© 1973 Punch

Bruce Petty

"He says he left his contact lenses in the glove compartment."

© 1974 Bruce Petty

James Stevenson

"How do you do? I'm the genie's agent."

Jules Stauber

© Jules Stauber

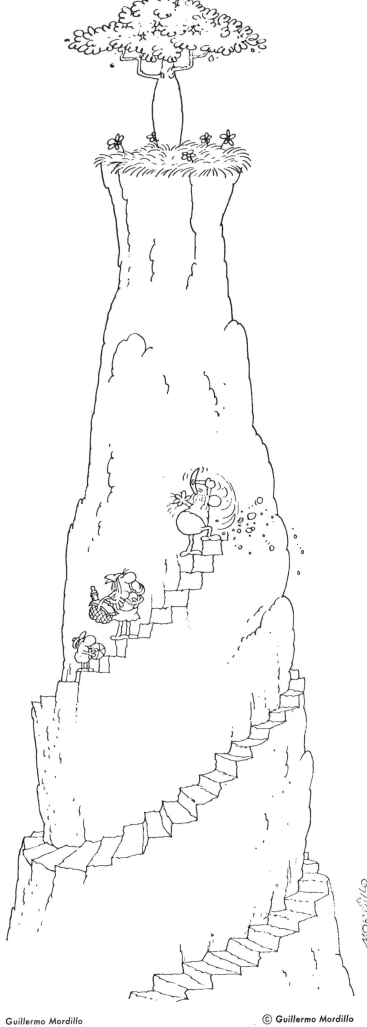

Guillermo Mordillo

© Guillermo Mordillo

"Well, I wouldn't exactly say that I've lost contact with the outside world."

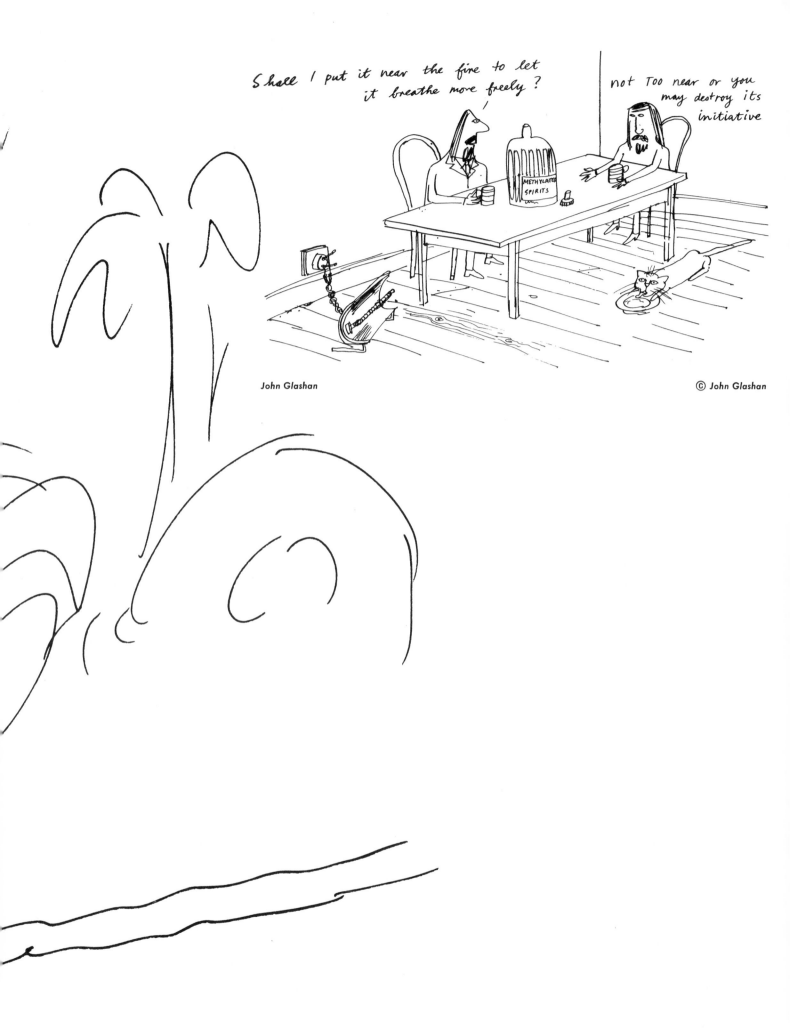

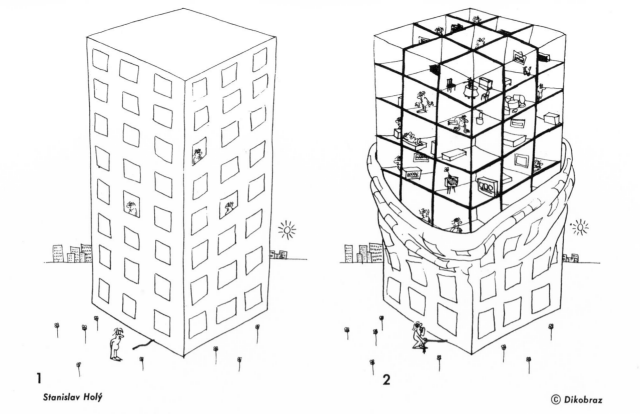

Stanislav Holý

© Dikobraz

1

2

Jules Stauber

© Jules Stauber

"Are you sure the gas gauge is working?"

1

2

Vladimír Renčín

3

Alex Graham   "You should have been firmer with him when he was a   © 1973 Punch
puppy!"

Leslie Starke

© 1973 The New Yorker

Jules Stauber